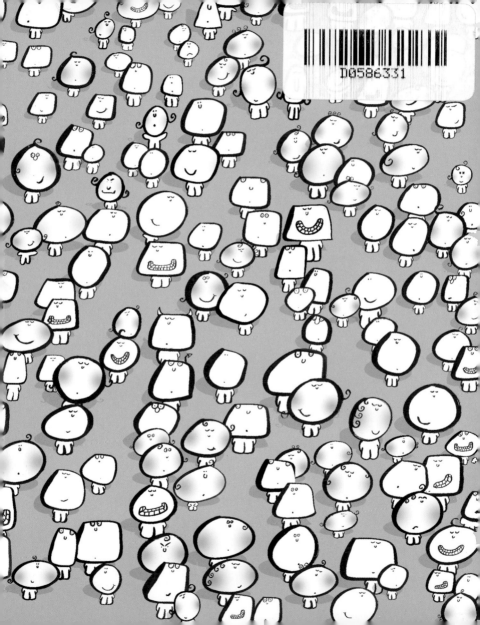

dogs

dogs

the answer to the universe is woof.

Vimrd **by Lisa Swerling and Ralph Lazar**

HarperCollins*Publishers*

i am so cute that
often i just want
to cuddle myself

convert to
dog

it's a lot nicer than
being **a people**

listen mister, i hate
to tell you this, but
you know the way you
shout when there's
a football match on tv,
well, **they can't
hear you**

the question is miaow?

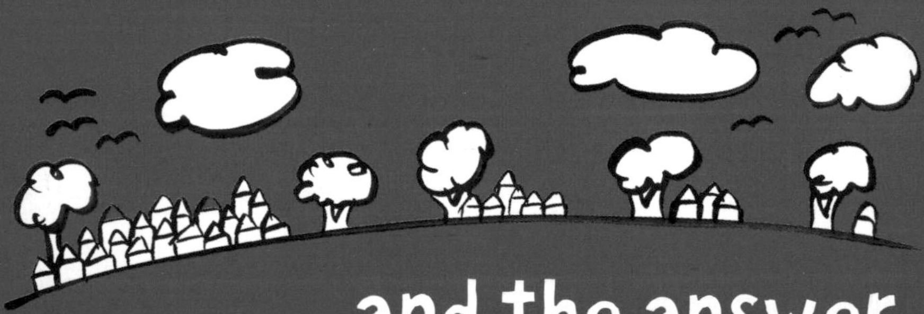

...and the answer is woof.

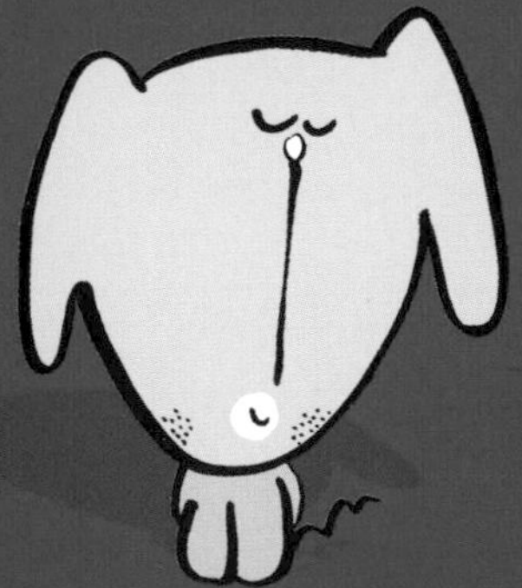

i had to choose between my

dog and my husband.

i do miss him sometimes, he was a good man.

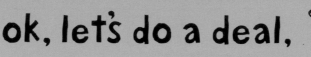
ok, let's do a deal,

you take
me for a
walk,

and i'll refrain
from crapping
on the carpets

i'm tired of barking.

i kind of wish i could speak.

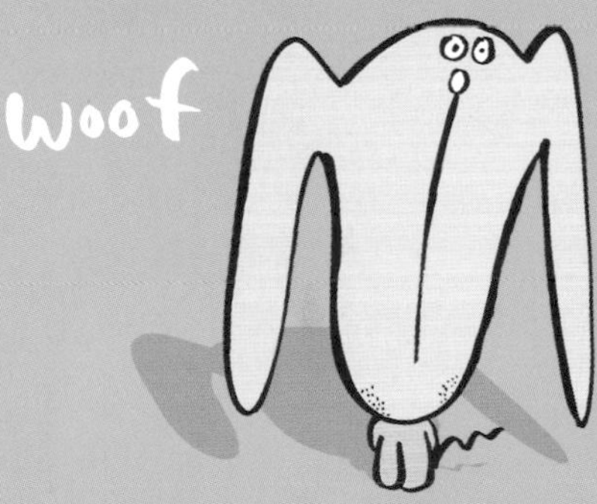

he's now gone and put up a sign that reads

beware of the dog

i'm not quite sure whether to take it as a compliment or as an insult?

try, try and
try again.
then rest, and then
try and try.
then rest.
then try.

then give
up.

behind every great dog, is a bumhole waiting to be sniffed.

never stand between a good dog and a good bone

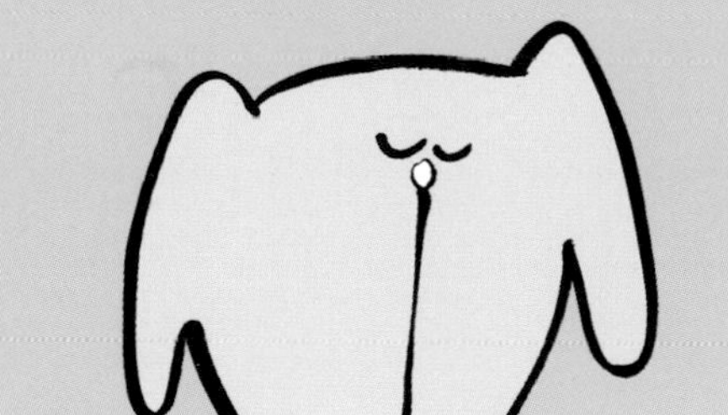

hello, this is your dog speaking.

you have no idea what you're doing, do you?

if you humans had
tails to wag you'd
be far less stressed,
i'm telling you...

i blame my owner

i am not obsessed with chasing sticks, i am not obsessed with chasing sticks, i am not obsessed with chasing sticks, i am not obsessed with chasing sticks, i am not obsessed with chasing sticks, i am not obsessed with chasing sticks...

ok, ok, it's safe to assume god is a dog, but what kind of dog?

the **more** i think about
life the more perplexing
i find it,

and the **less**
i think about it,
the more perplexing
i find it,

so what choice
do i have but to go
outside and take a
nap...

lisa swerling + ralph lazar

are two of the uk's most popular
graphic artists. through their company
last lemon they have brought to life a
range of inspired cartoon characters,
including harold's planet, the brainwaves,
blessthischick and, of course, vimrod.

they are married with two children,
and live in london.

HarperCollins*Publishers*

77–85 Fulham Palace Road, Hammersmith, London W6 8JB

www.harpercollins.co.uk

Published by HarperCollins*Publishers* 2008

2

Copyright © Lisa Swerling and Ralph Lazar 2008

The Authors assert the moral right to be identified as the authors of this work

A catalogue record for this book is available from the British Library

ISBN-10 0-00-728032-2

ISBN-13 978-0-00-728032-2

Set in Bokka

Printed and bound in China by Leo Paper Products

All rights reserved. No part of this publication may be reproduced,
stored in a retrieval system, or transmitted, in any form or by any means,
electronic, mechanical, photocopying, recording or otherwise,
without the prior permission of the publishers.

other titles in the **Vimrod** collection:

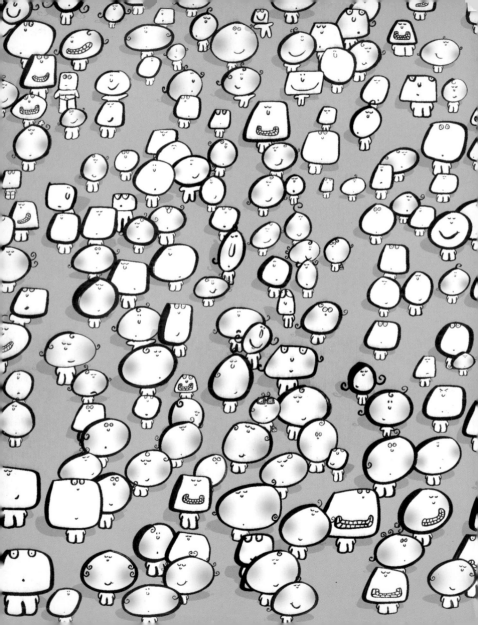